Business Marketing

Strategic Digital Marketing

Hina Victor

Business Marketing
Copyright © 2023 by Hina Victor

Printed in Pakistan by Hina

Dedication

In the realm of business, where potential open doors flourish and contest is savage, achievement isn't simply a question of possibility. It requires an immovable obligation to greatness, a significant comprehension of the steadily developing business sector scene, and an enduring devotion to the workmanship and study of business promoting.

To the visionary business visionaries who set out on this difficult excursion, I devote these words to celebrate the meaning of business showcasing. It is the backbone of any venture, the course that interfaces the essence of an item or administration with the personalities and wants of the interest group.

Commitment to business showcasing is a promise to develop and adjust to the moving tides of buyer conduct ceaselessly. It requests the resolute quest for figuring out the requirements, yearnings, and trouble spots of our clients. Compassion and knowledge are our directing signals in exploring the complicated snare of human feelings that impact buying choices.

We devote ourselves to the specialty of narrating, winding around stories that resound with our clients and make enduring impressions. From the convincing slogans to the dazzling visuals, each component turns into a brushstroke on the material of our image's character.

Business promoting flourishes with inventiveness and advancement, pushing us to break liberated from the limits of show. It moves us to think past the conventional limits, investigating new stages and advances that associate us with our crowd in remarkable ways.

We perceive the force of information and investigation, recognizing their job as the compass directing us towards information driven choices. Commitment to business promoting expects us to embrace these bits of knowledge as well as to change them into significant procedures that drive development and encourage long haul connections.

In this commitment, we recognize that showcasing is definitely not a singular undertaking yet an aggregate pursuit. It calls upon the cooperative endeavors of gifted people from different foundations, all cooperating as one to arrange crusades that reverberate with the world.

To the brand envoys, the advertisers, the promoters, the substance makers, and each individual from the showcasing local area, this commitment is a recognition for your energy and devotion. Your persistent quest for greatness fills the driving force of trade and hoists the actual embodiment of business.

May we keep on moving forward, outfitted with creativity and filled by a common obligation to greatness. Allow us to embrace change with great enthusiasm, for it is through advancement that we track down the best open doors.

This devotion is an update that in the domain of business promoting, achievement isn't estimated only by benefits yet by the enduring effect we make, the connections we support, and the heritages we abandon. As we set forth into unfamiliar waters, may our devotion to business promoting act as a directing light, enlightening our way to thriving and satisfaction.

Hina Victor

Table of Contents

Foreword

In the huge and dynamic universe of business, showcasing stands tall as a reference point of vital resourcefulness and imaginative ability. It is both a craftsmanship and a science, a fragile dance between understanding customer wants and creating convincing stories that enamor hearts and brains. As we leave on this investigation of business showcasing, I'm more than happy to acquaint you with a domain that revives items, administrations, and brands, giving them the wings to take off in the midst of an ocean of contenders.

In this steadily advancing scene, the job of showcasing has risen above simple ad and advancement. It has turned into the main impetus behind client commitment, faithfulness, and backing. Successful promoting pushes organizations higher than ever as well as manufactures profound associations with purchasers, changing exchanges into significant connections.

The pages ahead are a demonstration of the force of innovativeness, exploration, and development, where systems are made, and crusades are carefully intended to leave an enduring effect. We dive into the significance of statistical surveying, distinguishing the necessities and inclinations of buyers, and disentangling the secrets of their always evolving ways of behaving.

With the ascent of the computerized age, showcasing has gone through a change in perspective, opening new roads for organizations to associate with their crowds. We investigate the domain of computerized showcasing, from the complexities of site design improvement to the tremendous scenes of virtual entertainment and content advertising.

However, let us not fail to remember the immortal rules that stay the groundwork of powerful showcasing techniques. In these pages, we commend the quintessence of narrating, for a convincing story has the ability to rise above socioeconomics and contact the center of human feelings. We honor marking, perceiving that a strong brand personality can become inseparable from trust, dependability, and legitimacy.

As we venture through the profundities of promoting brain research, we reveal the unpretentious subtleties that impact direction, and we figure out how to use this information with moral obligation. For showcasing isn't just about influence; it is tied in with laying out validity and conveying certified worth to our clients.

Chasing advertising greatness, cooperation turns into a fundamental fixing. We investigate the meaning of collaboration and cooperative energy, as experts from different foundations join to make showcasing works of art that reverberate with worldwide crowds.

As you explore through the sections that follow, I urge you to embrace the soul of development and embrace the difficulties that lie ahead. For in the realm of business promoting, the excursion is just about as thrilling as the objective.

It is with extraordinary joy that I present to you this summary on business showcasing. May it act as a wellspring of motivation and information, lighting the enthusiasm inside you to make effective missions that make history.

Here's to the advertisers, the visionaries, and the trailblazers who shape the fate of business through their commitment, resourcefulness, and unfaltering quest for greatness.

Hina Victor

Preface

Welcome to the enrapturing universe of business showcasing, where imagination meets technique, and development interlaces with purchaser brain research. As you leave on this excursion, we welcome you to investigate the multi-layered domain of promoting that reinvigorates undertakings, drives brands higher than ever, and encourages enduring associations with clients.

In the pages that follow, we dive into the complexities of business showcasing, investigating its development from a simple device of advancement to a unique power that drives development and shapes the actual texture of trade. This summary fills in as an aide, revealing insight into the standards, strategies, and methods of reasoning that support effective promoting tries.

Part by section, we unwind the significance of understanding the market scene, leading thorough examination, and interpreting customer conduct. From recognizing undiscovered chances to foreseeing arising patterns, market experiences structure the bedrock of powerful showcasing techniques.

In the midst of the steadily changing advanced scene, we embrace the force of innovation and investigate the devices that engage advertisers to associate with their main interest groups across the globe. From tackling the capability of online entertainment stages to utilizing information driven investigation, we explore the advanced space that has re-imagined the manner in which organizations convey and draw in with shoppers.

All through this excursion, we give proper respect to the specialty of narrating, perceiving its significant effect on building profound associations and laying out brand personalities. We dig into the complexities of creating convincing stories that resound with assorted crowds and inhale legitimacy into brand messages.

Morals and obligation become the overwhelming focus as we investigate the fragile harmony among influence and certifiable worth creation. We underscore the significance of developing trust and straightforwardness with buyers, for a practical business flourishes with the faithfulness of its clients.

In the soul of cooperation, we commend the aggregate exertion of advertising groups, every part contributing their extraordinary ability to coordinate fruitful missions. From publicists and originators to information examiners and tacticians, together, they make orchestras of showcasing brightness.

As we explore the steadily developing promoting scene, we urge you to embrace change, flexibility, and a persistent quest for information. In reality as we know it where patterns arise and blur at lightning speed, a development outlook turns into an impetus for remaining on top of things.

This prelude makes way for an investigation that rises above the conventional limits of promoting. It is a challenge to set out on an extraordinary excursion that will furnish you with the devices, bits of knowledge, and motivation to influence the universe of business promoting.

We stretch out our genuine appreciation to every one of the givers, industry specialists, and thought pioneers who have shared their insight to improve this summary. Their aggregate skill fills in as a directing light, enlightening the way to showcasing greatness.

May this excursion through the domain of business promoting move you to embrace advancement, support imagination, and continue onward earnestly and energy. As you turn the pages, may you find the monstrous potential that advertising holds in molding organizations as well as the existences of those they contact.

Partake in the journey ahead, and may it impel you towards progress in the powerful universe of business advertising..

Introduction

In the quick moving and steadily developing universe of business, promoting assumes a significant part in driving achievement and forming the fate of ventures. As the scaffold between an organization and its clients, successful showcasing fills in as the compass that explores organizations through the wild waters of rivalry, development, and changing buyer requests.

The embodiment of business promoting lies in figuring out the longings, requirements, and goals of the interest group. It includes creating convincing stories that reverberate with individuals on a significant level, lighting feelings that lead to activity. Whether it's a global company, a neighborhood startup, or an independent business visionary, the standards of promoting stay widespread, directing organizations towards their objectives.

In this complete investigation of business promoting, we jump profound into the center ideas, techniques, and practices that characterize this unique discipline. From customary advertising to the progressive advanced scene, we shed light on the horde strategies that enable organizations to flourish and develop.

Part by section, we unwind the significance of statistical surveying, establishing the groundwork for informed navigation. We investigate the meaning of recognizing objective business sectors, dissecting contenders, and evaluating market patterns, empowering organizations to situate themselves decisively for progress.

As we adventure into the computerized age, we uncover the groundbreaking effect of advanced advertising. From website streamlining (Web optimization) to pay-per-click (PPC) publicizing, from online entertainment commitment to email showcasing, the computerized domain opens vast opportunities for organizations to draw in with a worldwide crowd.

Credibility and marking become the dominant focal point as we stress the meaning of building areas of strength for a character. A very much created brand conveys an organization's qualities and mission as well as encourages trust and dedication among shoppers.

Morals and social obligation are intertwined all through our investigation, helping us to remember the significant effect showcasing can have on people and society. Dependable promoting goes past benefit driven intentions, embracing a pledge to influence the existences of clients and the more noteworthy local area decidedly.

The excursion through business showcasing isn't without its difficulties. We address the impediments that advertisers face, for example, remaining in front of quickly changing purchaser patterns, utilizing information without compromising protection, and adjusting to the troublesome powers of innovation.

In the midst of these difficulties, we additionally commend the victories and triumphs of organizations that have saddled the force of promoting to make history. We share motivating contextual investigations and accounts of development that outline the extraordinary capability of compelling showcasing.

As we dive into the profundities of business showcasing, we welcome you to set out on this undertaking with a receptive outlook and a hunger for information. Whether you are a yearning advertiser, a carefully prepared entrepreneur, or essentially inquisitive about the workmanship and study of promoting, there is something for everybody in these pages.

May this excursion through the domain of business showcasing light your energy, flash imagination, and outfit you with the devices to succeed in the serious scene of trade. Together, let us unwind the secrets, commend the victories, and uncover the unlikely treasures that make business showcasing a steadily advancing and captivating pursuit.

In this way, moving along, let us set forth into the spellbinding universe of business advertising!

Hina Victor

Chapter 1
The Fundamentals of Business Marketing

In the huge and dynamic scene of business promoting, achievement isn't only an issue of chance however a consequence of painstakingly spread out procedures and a top to bottom comprehension of the central rules that support this dazzling discipline. This part fills in as a passage to the universe of business showcasing, laying the preparation for our investigation into the center ideas that drive development, cultivate associations, and shape the predetermination of endeavors.

1.1 Characterizing Business Advertising:

At its embodiment, business showcasing can be characterized as the most common way of advancing items, administrations, or brands to an interest group fully intent on satisfying client needs while accomplishing the association's targets. It goes past simple promoting and deals, enveloping a comprehensive methodology that includes statistical surveying, item improvement, valuing, dissemination, and client relationship the executives.

1.2 The Client Driven Approach:

A focal mainstay of viable promoting is the client driven approach, which rotates around setting the client at the core of all choices and activities. Grasping the requirements, inclinations, and trouble spots of the interest group is critical to making showcasing messages that impact them on a close to home level.

1.3 Statistical surveying and Examination:

Careful statistical surveying structures the bedrock of effective advertising efforts. By get-together and examining information about the business, contenders, and purchaser conduct, organizations can acquire important experiences that illuminate their procedures and separate them from the opposition.

1.4 Recognizing Objective Business sectors:

Projecting a wide net might appear to be engaging, however a laser-centered way to deal with recognizing objective business sectors yields improved results. Fitting advertising endeavors to explicit sections permits organizations to address the novel necessities and interests of various client bunches actually.

1.5 Structure Major areas of strength for a Character:

A strong brand personality goes past a logo and a slogan; it addresses the embodiment of an organization and a big motivator for it. Creating a convincing brand story and reliably following through on brand guarantees encourages trust and unwaveringness among purchasers.

1.6 The Advertising Blend:

The advertising blend involves the four Ps: Item, Value, Spot, and Advancement. Understanding how these components collaborate and impact each other empowers advertisers to think up even techniques that take care of client needs while amplifying business goals.

1.7 Coordinated Showcasing Interchanges:

A durable and incorporated promoting interchanges technique guarantees that all showcasing endeavors work amicably towards a shared objective. It includes synchronizing promoting, advertising, web-based entertainment, content showcasing, and different channels to convey a steady and brought together brand message.

1.8 Embracing the Advanced Scene:

In the present computerized age, organizations should adjust to the steadily changing web-based scene. From website improvement (Web optimization) to virtual entertainment showcasing and email crusades, computerized channels offer a plenty of chances to interface with a worldwide crowd.

1.9 Morals and Social Obligation:

Mindful advertising isn't just about productivity yet in addition about the effect on society and the climate. Embracing moral practices and corporate social obligation (CSR) can improve an organization's standing and fabricate enduring associations with clients.

1.10 Estimating Achievement:

Evaluating the progress of promoting endeavors is fundamental for consistent improvement. Key execution markers (KPIs) and examination assist organizations with evaluating the adequacy of their procedures and pursue information driven choices for future missions.

End:

As we close our investigation of the basics of business showcasing, we perceive that these standards lay the basis for every resulting section. Understanding and dominating these essentials enables advertisers and entrepreneurs the same to effectively explore the intricacies of the cutting edge commercial center. By embracing a client driven approach, utilizing information driven experiences, and adjusting to the computerized age, organizations can produce a way towards economical development and long haul achievement.

Chapter 2
Content Marketing Mastery

In the advanced period, content has turned into the money of association among organizations and their ideal interest groups. Content promoting is an essential methodology that spins around making and circulating important, pertinent, and reliable substance to draw in, connect with, and hold an obviously characterized crowd. This section digs into the workmanship and study of content advertising, investigating the methods and procedures that enable organizations to dominate this strong type of correspondence.

2.1 Grasping Substance Showcasing:

Content showcasing is something beyond making limited time material; it is tied in with conveying worth to the crowd. It includes creating content that teaches, engages, rouses, or tackles issues, situating organizations as legitimate and dependable sources inside their industry.

2.2 Characterizing Ideal interest group and Objectives:

Powerful satisfied showcasing begins with a profound comprehension of the interest group. By making purchaser personas and characterizing their necessities, inclinations, and trouble spots, organizations can tailor content that resounds with explicit portions. Furthermore, laying out clear objectives and targets gives guidance and inspiration to content endeavors.

2.3 Making Convincing Substance:

The progress of content promoting depends on the nature of the substance delivered. From blog entries and articles to recordings, infographics, digital broadcasts, and then some, organizations should put resources into making different and connecting with content that enthralls their crowd.

2.4 Embracing Narrating:

Narrating is an integral asset that rises above socioeconomics and contacts the hearts of people. By winding around stories that summon feelings and associate with the crowd's encounters, organizations can fashion further associations and have enduring effects.

2.5 Website improvement (Web optimization):

Advancing substance for web crawlers is crucial for expanding perceivability and drawing in natural rush hour gridlock. Understanding catchphrase research, on-page advancement, and third party referencing procedures can assist with satisfying position higher on web index results pages (SERPs).

2.6 Utilizing Web-based Entertainment:

Web-based entertainment stages give a tremendous and open crowd for content circulation. Organizations should distinguish the most pertinent channels for their crowd and make shareable substance that energizes commitment and brand backing.

2.7 Consolidating Video Showcasing:

Video content has seen remarkable development in prevalence. From short-structure recordings for online entertainment to long-frame instructive substance, video promoting permits organizations to pass on complex messages in a convincing and outwardly engaging way.

2.8 Drawing in Email Advertising:

Email stays an intense channel for sustaining leads and building client connections. Creating customized and designated email missions can drive changes and client faithfulness.

2.9 Estimating Content Showcasing Execution:

Examining the presentation of content promoting endeavors is fundamental for measure achievement and recognize regions for development. Measurements, for example, site traffic, transformation rates, time on page, and web-based entertainment commitment give significant bits of knowledge.

2.10 Adjusting to Arising Patterns:

The scene of content promoting is always advancing, with new innovations and stages continually arising. Keeping up to date with patterns and taking on creative methodologies guarantees that organizations stay important and serious.

End:

Content promoting is a dynamic and multi-layered discipline that enables organizations to interface really with their crowds. By figuring out the requirements of their objective clients and creating convincing, significant substance, organizations can develop connections, lay out power, and drive business development. As the computerized scene keeps on developing, content promoting dominance stays a critical point of support for progress in the steadily impacting universe of showcasing.

Chapter 3

Social Media Marketing Strategies

Online entertainment has changed the manner in which organizations associate with their crowds, turning into a fundamental apparatus for advertising in the computerized age. This part investigates the domain of virtual entertainment showcasing, divulging the systems and best practices that empower organizations to saddle the force of social stages to draw in, impact, and fabricate enduring associations with their objective clients.

3.1 Comprehension Web-based Entertainment Promoting:

Online entertainment advertising is the act of utilizing virtual entertainment stages to advance items, administrations, or brands and draw in with crowds. It includes making and sharing substance that resounds with supporters, directing people to sites, and cultivating significant associations.

3.2 Picking the Right Web-based Entertainment Stages:

Every online entertainment stage takes special care of various socioeconomics and client ways of behaving. Understanding the qualities and limits of stages like Facebook, Instagram, Twitter, LinkedIn, YouTube, and others is fundamental for choosing the most pertinent channels for arriving at the main interest group.

3.3 Making a Web-based Entertainment Showcasing Plan:

A very much organized online entertainment promoting plan frames objectives, ideal interest group, content system, posting recurrence, and key execution markers (KPIs). A durable arrangement guarantees that endeavors line up with business goals and yield quantifiable outcomes.

3.4 Connecting with Content Creation:

Convincing substance is at the core of fruitful online entertainment advertising. Visual components, for example, pictures and recordings, assume a huge part in catching consideration, while composed content should be compact, drawing in, and custom fitted to the inclinations of the stage's clients.

3.5 Utilizing Powerhouse Promoting:

Powerhouses, with their enormous and committed followings, can enhance a brand's message and increment reach. Working together with powerhouses who line up with a brand's qualities and main interest group can yield legitimate and significant organizations.

3.6 Local area The board:

Viable people group the board includes effectively captivating with devotees, answering remarks and messages expeditiously, and encouraging a feeling of having a place among the online entertainment local area. Building veritable associations with clients can prompt brand backing and unwaveringness.

3.7 Social Promoting:

Paid online entertainment publicizing permits organizations to target explicit socioeconomics, interests, and ways of behaving. Vital promotion missions can help brand mindfulness, drive traffic, and produce leads or transformations.

3.8 Virtual Entertainment Examination:

Virtual entertainment examination give significant experiences into crowd conduct, content execution, and in general mission viability. Examining measurements like commitment rates, navigate rates, and crowd socioeconomics advances methodologies for improved results.

3.9 Embracing Patterns and Virality:

Remaining sensitive to web-based entertainment patterns and viral substance permits organizations to partake in ideal discussions and profit by important themes. In any case, keeping up with realness and importance is essential to try not to seem astute.

3.10 Virtual Entertainment and Client support:

Web-based entertainment has turned into a conspicuous channel for client support communications. Tending to client requests and concerns instantly and graciously on friendly stages can upgrade a brand's standing and cultivate client devotion.

End:

Web-based entertainment showcasing has turned into an essential part of present day promoting procedures, giving organizations exceptional chances to interface with their crowds on an individual level. By creating connecting with content, utilizing social publicizing, and embracing virtual entertainment patterns, organizations can intensify their image's presence and effect on these unique stages. As web-based entertainment keeps on developing, adjusting and enhancing in this circle will stay central for organizations looking to flourish in the serious computerized scene.

Chapter 4

Search Engine Optimization (SEO) Unlocked

In the computerized period, web crawlers have turned into the doorway to the immense ocean of online data. Site improvement (Web optimization) is the workmanship and study of upgrading a site's perceivability in web search tool results, making it more available to clients looking for significant data. This section opens the complexities of Website design enhancement, digging into the methodologies and strategies that engage organizations to climb the positions and arrive at the sought after top situations in web crawler postings.

4.1 Figuring out Site design improvement:

Web optimization is the act of streamlining a site and its substance to rank higher in web search tool results pages (SERPs). It includes a blend of on-page and off-page systems intended to work on a site's pertinence and authority according to web crawlers.

4.2 The Significance of Watchwords:

Watchwords are the underpinning of Website design enhancement. Understanding the words and expressions clients use to look for data in a specific industry or specialty is fundamental for making significant and improved content.

4.3 On-Page Website design enhancement:

On-page Web optimization includes streamlining components straightforwardly on the site to work on its perceivability to web search tools. This incorporates improving title labels, meta depictions, headings, URL structures, and integrating significant watchwords inside the substance.

4.4 Excellent Substance:

Web crawlers esteem top caliber, important, and unique substance. Making far reaching, enlightening, and connecting with content draws in clients as well as signs position to web crawlers.

4.5 Specialized Search engine optimization:

Specialized Web optimization centers around the site's backend and execution, guaranteeing that web search tool crawlers can access and list the webpage productively. Appropriately organized site maps, quick stacking pages, versatile responsiveness, and secure HTTPS are indispensable parts of specialized Search engine optimization.

4.6 Off-Page Website design enhancement:

Off-page Web optimization includes factors outer to the site that impact its web search tool rankings. Fabricating excellent backlinks from legitimate and important sites, virtual entertainment sharing, and online notices add to a site's power and believability.

4.7 Nearby Website optimization:

For organizations with actual areas, nearby Web optimization is basic for showing up in neighborhood query items. Improving Google My Professional resources, guaranteeing Rest (Name, Address, Telephone Number) consistency, and collecting positive audits are urgent for neighborhood Website optimization achievement.

4.8 Voice Inquiry Enhancement:

The ascent of voice-actuated menial helpers has changed the manner in which clients look for data. Enhancing content for voice search includes understanding normal language questions and giving succinct and conversational responses.

4.9 Staying aware of Calculation Updates:

Web crawlers persistently update their calculations to furnish clients with the most pertinent and great outcomes. Remaining informed about these updates and adjusting Web optimization systems appropriately is fundamental for keeping up with rankings and perceivability.

4.10 Estimating Website design enhancement Achievement:

Checking and dissecting Web optimization execution is essential for following advancement and recognizing regions for development. Key measurements, like natural traffic, navigate rates (CTR), bob rates, and watchword rankings, give bits of knowledge into Web optimization viability.

End:

Opening the capability of Site design improvement is a consistent excursion of transformation, investigation, and enhancement. By grasping the complexities of on-page and off-page Website optimization, embracing great substance creation, and remaining informed about web crawler calculation refreshes, organizations can situate themselves for progress in the cutthroat advanced scene. As web crawlers develop, Web optimization stays an amazing asset for organizations trying to successfully improve their internet based perceivability and arrive at their ideal interest groups.

Chapter 5
Data-Driven Marketing

In the computerized age, information has arisen as a significant money that engages organizations to go with informed choices, figure out shopper conduct, and improve showcasing techniques. Information driven showcasing is the act of utilizing information and investigation to shape advertising drives, empowering organizations to convey customized encounters and make more significant levels of progress. This part dives into the universe of information driven advertising, investigating its importance, philosophies, and the significant effect it can have on business results.

5.1 The Force of Information in Showcasing:

Information is the soul of current advertising. It gives experiences into client inclinations, ways of behaving, and communications, empowering organizations to fit advertising endeavors to individual necessities and inclinations.

5.2 Gathering and Dissecting Information:

The course of information driven showcasing starts with gathering pertinent information from different sources. This incorporates client socioeconomics, site collaborations, virtual entertainment commitment, email cooperations, and that's only the tip of the iceberg. Dissecting this information utilizing different devices and procedures uncovers significant examples and patterns.

5.3 Client Division:

Information driven showcasing permits organizations to portion their client base into particular gatherings in view of shared attributes. These portions can then be designated with customized showcasing messages that reverberate with their particular advantages.

5.4 Personalization and Client Experience:

Personalization is a sign of information driven showcasing. By utilizing information bits of knowledge, organizations can make modified encounters that address individual inclinations, upgrading consumer loyalty and devotion.

5.5 Prescient Examination:

Prescient examination utilizes verifiable information to gauge future results and conduct. By utilizing prescient models, organizations can expect client needs, recognize possible stir, and advance showcasing lobbies for improved results.

5.6 A/B Testing and Enhancement:

Information driven showcasing depends on A/B testing and enhancement to refine promoting endeavors constantly. By testing various varieties of advertising components and breaking down execution information, organizations can recognize the best methodologies.

5.7 Advertising Mechanization:

Information driven advertising is improved by showcasing mechanization instruments that smooth out and customize promoting assignments. Mechanization permits organizations to sustain leads, trigger customized messages, and convey convenient messages in light of client conduct.

5.8 Information Protection and Security:

As information turns out to be more basic in advertising, it is principal to guarantee information protection and security.

Organizations should comply with information assurance guidelines and lay out strong safety efforts to defend client data.

5.9 Attribution Demonstrating:

Attribution demonstrating credits worth to various touchpoints in the client venture, assisting organizations with understanding the effect of each showcasing channel. Information driven attribution takes into account more precise conveyance of promoting financial plans.

5.10 Nonstop Improvement and Emphasis:

Information driven promoting is an iterative course of nonstop improvement. By breaking down information consistently and going with information driven choices, organizations can refine their methodologies and accomplish improved results over the long haul.

End:

Information driven promoting addresses a groundbreaking change in the realm of showcasing, empowering organizations to move past mystery and suppositions. By bridling the force of information and investigation, organizations can acquire a more profound comprehension of their clients, make customized encounters, and enhance showcasing endeavors for most extreme effect. In the time of information overflow, embracing information driven showcasing isn't simply a benefit; it is fundamental for remaining serious and important in the present always advancing business   sector   scene.

Chapter 6

Email Marketing Excellence

Email showcasing stays a foundation of computerized promoting techniques, giving organizations an immediate and individual channel to speak with their crowd. When executed with greatness, email advertising can drive commitment, sustain leads, and encourage client devotion. This part dives into the workmanship and study of email showcasing, investigating the systems, best practices, and procedures that enable organizations to accomplish greatness in their email crusades.

6.1 The Force of Email Advertising:

Email advertising keeps on being one of the best advanced promoting channels. It permits organizations to contact their crowd straightforwardly, convey customized content, and construct enduring associations with clients.

6.2 Structure and Sustaining an Email Rundown:

A top notch email list is the groundwork of effective email promoting. Organizations should zero in on building a natural and connected with list by offering important motivating forces and guaranteeing a consistent pick in process.

6.3 Division and Personalization:

Division separates the email list into explicit gatherings in light of shared qualities. By conveying customized content to each section, organizations can take special care of individual inclinations, bringing about higher commitment and change rates.

6.4 Creating Drawing in Email Content:

Convincing and important email content is critical to catching the beneficiary's consideration. From snappy titles to enlightening and outwardly engaging substance, every component adds to the general outcome of the email.

6.5 Robotized Email Missions:

Promoting computerization permits organizations to set off messages in view of explicit activities or occasions, like invite messages, deserted truck updates, and birthday good tidings. Mechanized crusades guarantee convenient and important communications with endorsers.

6.6 A/B Testing for Improvement:

A/B testing includes sending various forms of an email to subsets of the crowd to figure out which performs better. By testing components like titles, content, and invitations to take action, organizations can streamline their email lobbies for further developed results.

6.7 Guaranteeing Portable Responsiveness:

With the rising utilization of cell phones, messages should be advanced for versatile survey. Responsive email configuration guarantees that the substance is shown accurately across different gadgets, upgrading client experience.

6.8 Email Deliverability and Notoriety:

Keeping a positive source notoriety is vital for email deliverability. Organizations should stick to email showcasing best practices, screen bob rates, and stay away from nasty strategies to guarantee their messages land in supporters' inboxes.

6.9 Measurements and Email Execution:

Investigating email measurements, like open rates, navigate rates, and change rates, gives bits of knowledge into the viability of email crusades. Information driven investigation permits organizations to settle on information upheld choices for ceaseless improvement.

6.10 GDPR and Email Consistence:

Consenting to information security guidelines, like the Overall Information Assurance Guideline (GDPR), is fundamental for email showcasing. Organizations should acquire unequivocal assent from supporters, give clear quit choices, and handle information safely.

End:

Email showcasing greatness is a workmanship that requires a profound comprehension of crowd inclinations, convincing substance creation, and vital execution. By building a quality email list, conveying customized content, and utilizing computerization and investigation, organizations can excel at email showcasing and open its maximum capacity. In the steadily changing scene of computerized promoting, email stays an immortal and integral asset for drawing in with clients and driving business   development.

Chapter 7
Mobile Marketing Strategies

With the outstanding development of cell phone utilization, portable promoting has turned into a fundamental part of advanced advertising methodologies. Versatile advertising includes coming to and drawing in with crowds on their cell phones and tablets, conveying customized encounters that take special care of their in a hurry way of life. This part investigates the universe of portable promoting, disclosing the systems, strategies, and best practices that engage organizations to succeed in the versatile first time.

7.1 The Portable First Scene:

The expansion of cell phones has changed purchaser conduct, focusing on versatile advertising for organizations. Understanding the versatile first scene is fundamental for creating powerful portable advertising methodologies.

7.2 Portable Streamlined Sites:

A portable streamlined site guarantees that clients have a consistent and easy to use insight on their cell phones and tablets. Responsive plan, quick stacking times, and simple route are basic for drawing in versatile clients.

7.3 Portable Applications and In-Application Promoting:

Versatile applications give organizations an immediate and vivid channel to draw in with clients. In-application showcasing use message pop-ups, customized offers, and intuitive substance to upgrade client commitment and maintenance.

7.4 Area Based Advertising:

Area based advertising utilizes geolocation information to convey important and confined content to clients in view of their actual area. This technique is especially successful for organizations with actual areas or focusing on unambiguous geographic districts.

7.5 SMS and MMS Showcasing:

Short Message Administration (SMS) and Mixed media Informing Administration (MMS) are useful assets for direct correspondence with clients. Sending customized messages, advancements, and alarms by means of SMS/MMS can drive quick activity.

7.6 Versatile Promoting:

Versatile promoting envelops different configurations, including pennant advertisements, interstitials, local advertisements, and video advertisements. Versatile advertisements should be painstakingly focused on and subtle to offer some incentive to clients without upsetting their experience.

7.7 QR Codes and Versatile Responsive Substance:

QR codes empower clients to get to content or offers by filtering codes with their cell phones rapidly. Organizations can utilize QR codes to give extra data, unique advancements, or direct clients to portable streamlined presentation pages.

7.8 Portable Installment and Wallet Joining:

Working with portable installments and coordinating with computerized wallets like Mac Pay and Google Pay smoothes out the buying system for versatile clients, improving their comfort and driving transformations.

7.9 Web-based Entertainment and Versatile Commitment:

Web-based entertainment is vigorously gotten to through cell phones. Organizations should guarantee that their web-based entertainment content and commitment procedures are streamlined for versatile clients to expand their scope and association.

7.10 Dissecting Versatile Investigation:

Portable investigation gives experiences into client conduct, application use, and versatile mission execution. Examining versatile information permits organizations to refine their portable showcasing methodologies for improved results.

End:

Portable promoting procedures are fundamental for organizations trying to satisfy the needs of the present versatile driven buyers. From portable advanced sites and applications to area based showcasing and versatile publicizing, embracing versatile advertising opens up new roads for drawing in and associating with crowds. By utilizing the force of cell phones, organizations can convey customized encounters that reverberate with clients continuously, driving brand devotion and business development in the portable first period

Chapter 8
Influencer Marketing Secrets

In the period of virtual entertainment predominance, powerhouse promoting has arisen as a strong technique for organizations to interface with their ideal interest groups. Powerhouses, with their committed and drew in followings, have the capacity to impact shopper conduct and influence buying choices. This section discloses the key to effective force to be reckoned with advertising, investigating the systems, tips, and best practices that engage organizations to tackle the capability of powerhouses and accomplish significant outcomes.

8.1 Figuring out Powerhouse Advertising:

Powerhouse promoting includes working together with people who have a huge internet following and can influence the feelings and buying choices of their crowd. It is a cutting edge type of verbal exchange showcasing, enhanced through the force of virtual entertainment.

8.2 Distinguishing the Right Forces to be reckoned with:

Finding the right powerhouses for a brand is urgent for a fruitful powerhouse promoting effort. Organizations should consider factors like specialty pertinence, crowd socioeconomics, commitment rates, and brand arrangement while choosing powerhouses.

8.3 Miniature Powerhouses versus Full scale Powerhouses:

Miniature powerhouses are people with more modest however exceptionally drew in followings, while large scale powerhouses have a huge reach. The two classifications offer exceptional benefits, and the decision relies upon the mission's goals and interest group.

8.4 Structure Valid Connections:

Effective powerhouse advertising is based on legitimate and authentic connections among brands and forces to be reckoned with. Organizations ought to move toward powerhouses with truthfulness, straightforwardness, and a common vision for the mission.

8.5 Utilizing Client Created Content (UGC):

Empowering powerhouses and their supporters to make and share client created content connected with the brand or item cultivates validness and social verification. UGC upgrades brand validity and draws in additional shoppers.

8.6 Setting Clear Targets:

Characterizing clear targets and KPIs is fundamental for estimating the outcome of a powerhouse showcasing effort. Whether it's rising image mindfulness, driving site traffic, or helping deals, having explicit objectives directs the whole interaction.

8.7 Making Connecting with Content:

Teaming up with powerhouses to make convincing and drawing in happy is at the core of powerhouse showcasing. Content ought to line up with the powerhouse's style and resound with their crowd for most extreme effect.

8.8 Observing and Estimating Execution:

Following the exhibition of a powerhouse advertising effort is significant for evaluating its viability. Measurements like reach, commitment, navigate rates, and transformation rates give significant bits of knowledge into the mission's prosperity.

8.9 Exposures and Consistence:

Consistence with powerhouse showcasing guidelines, like revelation necessities for supported content, is imperative for keeping up with straightforwardness and believability. Organizations should guarantee that powerhouses uncover supported associations obviously.

8.10 Long haul Connections:

Constructing long haul associations with powerhouses can prompt more legitimate and significant missions. Laying out trust and sustaining joint efforts over the long haul considers further associations with crowds.

End:

Powerhouse showcasing can possibly lift a brand's perceivability, validity, and commitment to the computerized scene. By understanding the key to fruitful powerhouse advertising, organizations can explore this unique domain with certainty and accomplish surprising outcomes. Utilizing the force of powerhouses to make bona fide content and draw in with interest groups can be the impetus for driving brand dependability, extending reach, and driving business development in the period of virtual entertainment impact.

Chapter 9

Customer Experience (CX) Revolution:

In an undeniably serious business scene, the client experience (CX) has arisen as a characterizing factor that separates fruitful organizations from the rest. The CX upset rotates around making significant, customized, and consistent collaborations with clients at each touchpoint. This section investigates the client experience insurgency, uncovering the procedures, standards, and best practices that enable organizations to hoist their CX and construct enduring associations with their clients.

9.1 Comprehension Client Experience (CX):

Client experience incorporates each connection a client has with a brand all through their whole process - from beginning attention to post-buy support. It is the amount of all insights, feelings, and experiences that shape a client's relationship with a business.

9.2 The Job of Client Centricity:

A client driven approach puts the client at the core of all business choices. Understanding and expecting client needs and inclinations is fundamental for making extraordinary encounters that amuse clients.

9.3 Planning the Client Excursion:

Client venture planning includes imagining and seeing each phase of the client's insight. Planning recognizes problem areas, valuable open doors for development, and touchpoints where customized collaborations can be conveyed.

9.4 Personalization and Customization:

Personalization is a vital driver of the CX unrest. Using information bits of knowledge, organizations can convey redid encounters custom-made to individual inclinations, expanding consumer loyalty and devotion.

9.5 Consistent Omnichannel Encounters:

The CX unrest requires conveying a reliable and consistent experience across all channels and gadgets. Incorporating on the web and disconnected touchpoints guarantees a firm excursion for clients.

9.6 Enabling Client Commitment:

Connecting with clients in two-manner discussions cultivates a feeling of local area and brand dedication. Organizations can use web-based entertainment, live visit, reviews, and client input to engage client commitment.

9.7 Tackling the Force of man-made intelligence and Mechanization:

Man-made brainpower (computer based intelligence) and mechanization improve CX by offering ongoing help, customized suggestions, and smoothing out processes. Artificial intelligence driven chatbots and menial helpers improve client care and accommodation.

9.8 Sympathy and Profound Association:

Building a profound association with clients makes enduring impressions and drives brand support. Showing compassion, understanding, and appreciation in client cooperations cultivates compelling close to home bonds.

9.9 Proactive Client service:

Proactively tending to client issues and worries before they raise grandstands a business' devotion to consumer loyalty. Expecting client needs and it is fundamental to give quick goals.

9.10 Estimating and Working on CX:

Estimating CX measurements, for example, Net Advertiser Score (NPS), Consumer loyalty (CSAT), and Client Exertion Score (CES), permits organizations to check client feeling and recognize regions for development.

End:

The CX unrest has reshaped the manner in which organizations connect with their clients, setting consumer loyalty and unwaveringness at the very front of achievement. By embracing a client driven approach, utilizing personalization and innovation, and focusing on consistent encounters, organizations can lead the CX upset and make noteworthy minutes that reverberate with clients. In a period where client assumptions keep on rising, the CX upheaval becomes an upper hand as well as a central need for organizations looking to flourish and succeed in the hearts and brains of their clients.

Chapter 10
Sustainable Marketing Practices

As the world turns out to be progressively mindful of natural and social difficulties, supportable promoting rehearses have acquired critical significance. Supportable advertising goes past benefit driven intentions, underlining the obligation of organizations to limit their natural effect, advance social prosperity, and maintain moral qualities. This section investigates the domain of manageable promoting works on, uncovering the techniques, standards, and best practices that enable organizations to embrace supportability and contribute emphatically to society and the planet.

10.1 Characterizing Maintainable Advertising:

Maintainable showcasing, otherwise called green advertising or moral promoting, rotates around advancing items and administrations in a way that lines up with natural and social obligation. It includes making an incentive for clients while limiting adverse consequences on the climate and society.

10.2 The Triple Primary concern:

The idea of the triple primary concern thinks about three critical components of business achievement: individuals, planet, and benefit. Practical showcasing plans to offset financial success with social and ecological obligation.

10.3 Embracing Corporate Social Obligation (CSR):

Corporate Social Obligation includes organizations willfully making moves that benefit society past their monetary commitments. Adjusting promoting endeavors to CSR drives grandstands a promise to having a constructive outcome.

10.4 Straightforward and Genuine Correspondence:

Genuineness and straightforwardness are fundamental in economical promoting. Organizations should convey their maintainability endeavors honestly, staying away from greenwashing and guaranteeing arrangement among cases and activities.

10.5 Green Item Improvement:

Creating eco-accommodating and feasible items is a foundation of maintainable showcasing. By focusing on earth cognizant materials and assembling processes, organizations can offer greener options in contrast to purchasers.

10.6 Bundling and Waste Decrease:

Feasible bundling and waste decrease are basic parts of maintainable showcasing. Taking on eco-accommodating bundling materials and advancing reusing drives show natural stewardship.

10.7 Energy Proficiency and Carbon Impression:

Organizations can lessen their carbon impression by focusing on energy effectiveness, embracing sustainable power sources, and balancing discharges. Conveying endeavors to lessen natural effect constructs brand trust.

10.8 Mindful Store network The executives:

Supportable showcasing reaches out to inventory network rehearses. Organizations should guarantee moral obtaining, fair work rehearses, and capable provider associations to advance social prosperity.

10.9 Green Advertising Efforts:

Green advertising efforts bring issues to light about ecological issues and rouse positive activities. Organizations can involve narrating and online entertainment to draw in shoppers in feasible drives.

10.10 Long haul Responsibility:

Maintainable showcasing is definitely not a transient pattern yet a drawn out obligation to social and natural obligation. Consistently working on reasonable practices and drawing in partners encourages enduring effect.

End:

Feasible showcasing rehearses mark a change in outlook in the realm of business, underlining the interconnectedness between benefit, social effect, and natural stewardship. By embracing feasible showcasing, organizations can construct trust, reliability, and support among cognizant customers, adding to a better planet and a more fair society. The excursion towards manageability requires devotion, development, and coordinated effort, however the prizes are extensive, leaving a positive heritage for people in the future and guaranteeing a more splendid and more economical future.

www.ingramcontent.com/pod-product-compliance
Lightning Source LLC
Chambersburg PA
CBHW062302290526
45794CB00006B/2661